Jubilant

A Poetry Journey

By

Mitchell Adams

Barbara L. Adams

Table of Contents

Dedication

We dedicate this book to Jon, our husband/dad, who has always been supportive in all our endeavors. We love you.

Acknowledgments

We are extremely grateful to two amazing past teaching colleagues, Clare Telleen and Kyle Voeller, for editing and giving helpful feedback. We'd also like to give a shout-out to all the teachers and friends over the years who helped us with knowledge and insight. Finally, thank you, the reader, for taking the time to enjoy our verses.

About the Author

Barbara L. Adams is originally from Maine, spent decades in California, and now resides in Oregon. She is a retired English and Social Studies teacher and drew from that experience to craft her poetry styles. Volunteering, writing, traveling, and watching sports with her husband, son, and puppies are what she enjoys doing.

Mitchell Adams is an aspiring artist with a journalism degree. His experience in sales, writing music and scripts, have shaped his poetry journey. Born and raised in California, Mitchell's writing is intended to resonate with his peers while providing perspectives for all generations.

Genre: I am 25 words

Theme: Perception

"the balcony"

I am the balcony of a condo

inviting, therapeutic for those

who need some fresh air

sometimes, overcrowded

but the door will always remain open

Genre: I Am 25 Words

Theme: Perception

"Illuminate"

I am the sun breaking through the clouds. Warm rays can shine on you and illuminate

the way through the mist. Light triumphs over darkness.

Genre: you are 25 words

Theme: Perception

"the beach"

you are the calming currents by the beach

providing serenity in a safe space

warm sand, resembling a freckled face

still searching; just a mirage

Genre: You Are 25 Words

Theme: Perception

"Branches"

You are the oak tree in the forest. Standing tall, you protect and calm me during times of change. I love your strength, your shelter.

genre: free verse

theme: trust

"mystery"

girl, you are a mystery

how you feel about me
how you feel about me

girl, it's still a mystery

chillin' with my feels
in misery
speaking up
then we history

girl, you are a mystery
how you feel about me
how you feel about me
she keeps it to herself

Genre: Free Verse

Theme: Trust

"Palette"

We are foot soldiers protecting the inner castle,
the fortress of our hearts.
We are impressionist painters,
blending colors to make a palette of memories.
We are clumsy weavers,
creating a cloak to hide ourselves in.
We are patient gardeners,
planting and nurturing the seeds of love.
You are the music in my life,
the soundtrack of our memories.
You are my Gemini, two sides of the same person,
unpredictable yet constant.
You are my Best Friend, my confidant,
the keeper of my soul, my love for eternity.
You are my surprises,
my deep breaths - 1, 2, 3 - look at the ocean-sharer.
I am your sunshine, your bride, your Best Girl, your love.

Thank you for guarding my trust, for without it, this life
would not be possible.

genre: free verse
theme: trust

"undone"

trust
break it
start from scratch
itching to earn it back

patience
when you think it's close
it's not even close
like a shooting star out of reach

desperate
old habits die hard
denial is one of them
accusation is another

fragile
shattered pieces can't be fixed
stop lying to yourself
what is done will never be undone

Genre: Free Verse
Theme: Trust

"Twine"

Trust = firm belief in character, strength or truth of someone or something

I put my trust in you, and in return, you threw it away like an unnecessary burden.
The world imploded from within
like so many grains of sand,
washed out to sea, leaving
the forever dream now in ruins.

I put my trust in you, and in return, you blindsided me with searing pain.
Tears fell from her clouded eyes
she cried - it must be her fault,
her strong heart becoming fractured with anger and disbelief
that the Rockwell painting she carried with her had dimmed.

I put my trust in you, and in return, you made me question myself.
What was once confidence became questions with no answers.
What was once a fortified foundation became splinters and rubble.

What was once on a pedestal became a valley filled with
broken glass.

I put my trust in myself to leave and begin again.
If trust can be thrown away, it can also be gathered up in
piles with twine
to be stacked and built again.

genre: villanelle
theme: respect

"blind"

blind, the eye of the storm
spectacular spectacles cure
vision within starts to take form

jealousy is not the norm
for a heart that is pure
blind, the eye of the storm

secrets spread talking college dorms
don't let false narratives blur
vision within starts to take form

what was frozen is now warm
lens grasping, clarity occurs
blind, the eye of the storm

setbacks sting, watch the hornets swarm
hunting for knowledge so evil can't lure
vision within starts to take form

staring into space, a new galaxy is born
witness the progress, what's next, not sure
blind, the eye of the storm
vision within starts to take form

Genre: Villanelle
Topic: Respect

"Plea"

Hear each other instead of listen, I plea.
People are angry, and values are bid farewell
and we need more respect for you and me.

It's much too late to just let it all be,
with the kids living in their own hell.
Hear each other instead of listen, I plea.

Some parents don't teach them to think with empathy.
Past society's standards of values don't ring a bell,
and we need more respect for you and me.

Practicing and perfecting the Golden Rule is the key.
Understanding different perspectives, as well.

Hear each other instead of listen, I plea.

Social media is a killer of decency.
Lessons learned; only time will tell
and we need more respect for you and me.

Plant the seeds to grow the tree,
the house of kindness I will dwell.
Hear each other instead of listen, I plea,
and we need more respect for you and me.

poem: villanelle
theme: respect

"space"

you are not someone I need to impress
tank on empty, stealing what I need to fill
energy toxic, no more friends who depress

give me the space to decompress
wasting time in this Arctic cold world, need to chill
you are not someone I need to impress

words stuck like a traffic jam drives stress
kindness remains the weapon to kill
energy toxic, no more friends who depress

amnesia takes over, keep forgetting to dress
the burden is bitter, but I swallow the pill
you are not someone I need to impress

feel the pressure like a full-court press
ball in your court, but the movement is still
energy toxic, no more friends who depress

more to gain without, won't settle for less
gave my two cents but expected dollar bills
you are not someone I need to impress
energy toxic, no more friends who depress

Genre: Villanelle
Theme: Respect

"Bark or Peeling"

The tree of respect is tall and wide
with truths running dark and deep,
and esteem, like bark, is peeling from the sides.

She harbored hope that time would hide
the scars on her body like grains of sand.
The tree of respect is tall and wide.

On his love, she had always relied,
but what happens when fists start to land,
and esteem, like bark, is peeling from the sides.

In the hospital, she nearly died.
It's there where she decided to take a stand.
The tree of respect is tall and wide.

Within her broken soul, she summoned pride.
To be proud and confident, she planned,
though esteem, like bark, is peeling from the sides.

"I choose myself," she cried, "and let those who try to crush
me be damned!"
The tree of respect is tall and wide,
with esteem, like bark, peeling from the sides.

14

Genre: Acrostic
Theme: Friendship

"companion"

cannot go a day without communicating
only her I am sharing my secrets
my Mondays improve when talking to her
please, a word that holds vulnerable weight
and when the storm hits hard with rain
no burden of hers will be too heavy
I am here in confidence to hold
owning up to our mistakes is survival
never lacking accountability and honesty

Genre: Acrostic
Theme: Friendship

"Friends Part I"

Following no one around the school
Rejected and, worse yet, undetected
Invisible - like feeling alone in a crowd of people
Elsie ate lunch where not even the grasses would grow
No friends, no smiles, no secrets to share
"Do you want to hang out?" his eyes asked as she
Shyly walked over and said, "Hi."

poem: acrostic
theme: friendship

"journey"

just think of the very first moment
overtime still vivid like movies in imax
us in a memory filled with laughter
remembering how far we have come since
not close to the long-lasting journey's end
even when we go days without talking
you always resonate as a happy place

Genre: Acrostic
Theme: Friendship

"Friends Part II"

Friends are like the icing on a homemade cake
Rich in flavor, reliable when needed, ready to bring a smile
Inspiring me to be myself, be strong, be positive
Even with imperfections, we all admit
No one is an island; no one will
Drown in sorrow on my watch
Sharing life's bitter times and sweet desserts

genre: haiku
theme: love

"detachment"

detachment is bliss,
and within the lies is truth
detachment is peace

Genre: Haiku
Theme: Love

"Sunshine"

Constantly changing
Yet comfortingly, the same
You are my sunshine

genre: haiku
theme: love

"serenity"

heart stolen but safe
sanctuary in silence
space, serenity

Genre: Haiku
Theme: Love

"Precious"

My pets are the best
Furry friends forever heal
With adoration

genre: poem of 10 ones
theme: fear

"fear of love"

define forever
me and you
explain_eternity
some things are unexplainable

what about timing?
can't overemphasize importance
love contains no manipulation,
gentle calmness of comfort

how does one know
obvious as a sunny day
or is it just the imagination

Genre: Poem of 10 Ones
Theme: Fear

"Sting"

A dried brown nest
A high-pitched buzzing sound
A glimmer of gold
Making a working home

An unsuspecting human
Disrupts the scene
A pulse rises as sprinting begins

Into the lake, the runner ran
Hoping to quell the terror

genre: poems of 10 ones
theme: fears

"anxiety"

suffocating free fall
from meaningless words
gasping, inhaling then

exhaling insecurities

broken and shattered
let the mirror reflect
no comfort in the skin
like a snake shed it off

encouraging energy
sparks ignite
burning all anxiety

"Dawn"

A turbulent ocean
A sudden twig snaps
A lonely heart
Walks on the tracks

A frightened soul
Lives with uncertainty
A sunrise arises
Pushing her forward

Out of the darkness
The brave walk forth
On the path of resiliency

genre: internal rhyming
theme: loneliness

"knee-deep"

when they ask about fear, do they think that it's near
sound the alarms and ring the bells
do they know that it's here, clarity crystal clear
mirages of heaven disguise hell

disconnected like calls, who picks up when it falls
no more room in this dark place; what's love without
a face
like a blind old man, I can never tell

keep to myself, please keep, keep to myself can't
sleep
feel forced into sorrow only choice is to dwell
closed eyes count the sheep, where is myself knee-
deep
like a mime center stage, I won't ever tell

Genre: Internal Rhyming
Theme: Loneliness

"Change"

What to do to fill the unavoidable void,
No longer long-time employed.
No longer in a predictable routine.
Flailing like an inflatable wind puppet,
Friendless, endless, alone, unseen.

Reaching out, some reaching back,
I know it's about more than that, so
I moved, I'm missed, I miss
Decades of familiar friendships.

But as the sun arises, so does a new day
To find a way for you to stay
And be my friend.
Out of isolation and into the light;
Out of the darkness, I put up a fight.

genre: internal rhyme
theme: loneliness

"no response"

chasing to fill the void, permanently employed
no love filling up these empty friendships
alone in the golden state, strength in numbers holds
no weight
no trust filling up these empty friendships
doubt lingers like odor, can't spend a day sober
only option of peace I fear is the loner
silence is the friend who gives no response
you are the enemy who needs no response

Genre: Internal Rhyme
Theme: Loneliness

"Beacon"

Being alone and lonely are two different beasts.
The two can overlap or solely
Be unique in their subtle
Differences.
But it's the loneliness that begs a heart,
A heaven, a start, a light -
Anything to indicate or vindicate
That one's own existence matters-
That one's own light shines-
That one's own soul matters.
Isolation and sadness lead to
Desolation and madness.
We were made to crave human contact,
But this requires bravery for some.
So take a step.
Take a chance.
Take matters into your own hands.
Be that bright light.

genre: here, there poem
theme: societal issues

"american greed"

rent here
bills there
credit, payments everywhere

minimal stack counting
financial debt mounting
selfish budget sharing
and millionaire lifestyle wishing

dreams over the budget
tears behind the face
friends among the poor
and greed along the way

frustration here
tension there
money, prices everywhere

"Earth's Tears"

Conservationists here,
Lawmakers there,
Fire, drought everywhere.

Fossil fuels burning,
More people carpooling,
Extraordinary temperatures freezing,
and conscientious people worrying.

Smoke over the hills,
Plastics in the bins,
Animals on the run,
and changes in the house.

Policies here,
Conversions there,
Hope, recyclables everywhere.

genre: here, there poem
theme: societal issues

"american malice"

animosity here
confusion there
apathy silence everywhere

eccentric egos blinding
habitual lights flickering
ridiculous rhetoric regurgitating
and spiteful tweets, exhausting

hatred under the depths
agendas under the radar
evil in their hearts
and white supremacy on the line

stereotypes here
anti-semitism there
malice blood everywhere

"Grace"

Insecurity here,
Education there,
Protests, changes everywhere.

Young people sharing,
Helpful teachers listening,
Overwhelmed adults talking,
And new policies starting.

Marches along the street,
Psychologists in the office,
Truths of the heart,
And woe under the smiles.

Hope here,
Challenges there,
Questions, support everywhere.

"kings"

there once was a player for the kings
who visioned winning chips and rings
when it matters most, he swishes
lights out like birthday wishes
crowd like a choir as it cheers and sings

Genre: Limerick
Theme: Satirical

"Strike"

There once was a large man from Eugene,
Whose legal last name was Golean.
He got up to bat,
Caught the ball in his hat,
And ran away with girlfriend, Serene.

"elephant"

what a funny little animal the elephant
whose memory span makes it quite
intelligent
its trunk can lift over 700 pounds
rumbling and trumpeting type of sounds
makes the elephant in the room never
irrelevant

Genre: Limerick
Theme: Satirical

"Shenanigans"

There once was a small dog from Tracy,
Whose old master's name was Spacey.
They ran on the hedge,
And fell off the ledge,
And laughed at a cat named Lacey.

genre: sonnet
theme: seasons - winter

"invisible auroras"

cascades of piercing powder peacefully
rest amongst the grayish glacier granite
blankets of warm comfort, ease sleepily
calm the restless mute, the mind of manic

unexplainable landscapes, lake lagoons
rewards of refreshing relaxation
too much "not enough time" leaving too soon
shots hurt like hot vast venom, vacation

marvelous moose dance with wolves of the wise
near death experience, escape the freeze
whispers from the wind, warning the sunrise
mountain top deep breaths, barely feel the breeze

avoid the avalanche; treading lightly
invisible, northern lights shine brightly

Genre: Sonnet - Fall
Theme: Seasons

"Equinox"

It is more than just a season between
Summer and winter; it is an array
Of trees shedding their clothes, making a scene,
Piling up colors to rake in a day.

Amazing grapes, amazing grace, we hope,
Ripening on the vine, we are golden.
Facing the autumn of our lives, we cope,
Remember, time refused to be stolen.

Bats, brooms, bags bringing sweet treats in the dark,
In these childhood rituals, there's comfort.
Eating pumpkin pie at the harvest park,
Reminds us that each season is too short.

To each moment, we must of ourselves, give
So that we teach our children how to live.

genre: sonnet
theme: seasons - summer

"favorite pastime"

ice cubes blend like a vocal serenade
toast to accomplishments, as sunlight sways
attitudes sweet with sour lemonade
cheers echo like it's one of them good days

baseball grass pleasing to the naked eye
grills sizzle like an egg on the sidewalk
good nights cut short, no fun to say goodbye
earth, slow down; let mother nature's mind talk

grandma's organ, coliseum music
family and friends always invited
no school tomorrow or next, like too sick
sky resembles star wars films, excited

nothing better than drama, popcorn, please
swing and a miss, winning brings the most peace

Genre: Sonnet - Spring
Theme: Seasons

"Florence"

He grew flowers, hydrangeas, daffodils;
Her favorites, those remembrances of
Quiet hand-in-hand walks on the green hills,
Both hearts enjoying their season of love.

But the winter cold had ripped her from him;
Happiness was buried under the snow;
Gone too soon, his broken heart was now dim,
When would joy again, like real true love, flow?

The ice thawed, and hope sprung eternally,
Over mountains and in his warming heart.
Time of renewal was now he would heed,
The promise of a new love, not to part.

Like the Renaissance, focus on re-birth;
The springtime offers hope of joy and mirth.

Genre: cinquain
Theme: aging

"grizzled"

infant
to twenties
growing, maturing, adulting
blink of an eye,
grizzled

Genre: Cinquain
Theme: Aging

"Reminisce"

People
Heartful gathering
Aging, complaining, reliving
Time's a ruthless thief
Mortal

Genre: cinquain
Theme: aging

"moments before"

delusional
memory lost
embracing, fulfilling, unknowing
direction beyond the comprehension
flatline

Genre: Cinquain
Theme: Aging

"Twilight"

Twilight
Sails soon
Trying, learning, growing
Rowing as its captain
Steer

Poem: reverse poem
Theme: life

Reverse Poem Directions: Read the first time from top to bottom. Some lines carry on to the next line. Then read from bottom to top for the opposite meaning

"pressure"

I feel this necessary pressure amounting
not a fair statement I am making
life is about the journey, not the destination
manifesting takes one step at a time
I am sure that things will work in my favor
wrong decisions are being made and
indecisiveness will be the death of me, please
you decide what is right or wrong
can't seem to show up when it matters most
unreliable
is what they think of you
dependable
true statement
hear me out
life has been full of riches, but
no luck yet on the pot of gold
settling for the silver medal
winning is the only option
failure is the consistent result
I take pride in working hard and

accomplishments written on the bare wall
always stay humble
slowly losing control of the ego and
it's as toxic as a poison dart-frog
when you speak of my name
respectable words are communicated
clearly, there is no authenticity
makes it difficult to believe that
driving on the road to success
packing my bags like I'm ready to leave

Genre: Reverse Poem
Theme: Life

"Imperfection"

I am weighed down by unwanted expectations
And I refuse to believe that
Everyone's eyes are not on me
I realize this may be hard to understand, but
Thinking I can be perfect
Is a lie due to
Lack of opportunities
As time goes on, you will see that
I don't have my priorities straight because
Negativity
Is more important than
Optimism
I believed
Once upon a time
Life was simpler
But this will not be true in your era
The storms have washed out the rainbows
Experience tells me
Attitudes will not improve
I do not conclude that
Joy will be like a soothing cup of tea
In the future,
The flame will flicker out
No longer can it be said that

Everyone's eyes are understanding
It will be clear that defeat is inevitable
It is foolish to presume that
I will be without flaws
And all of this will come true unless I reverse it

Genre: reverse poem
Theme: life

"amends"

when drawing the line, I am out of ink
I can't erase what has been scarred
wounds heal over precious time
I am negligent with the healing process, but
give me some space to think it over
clarity can be a mirage
we don't have the same vision
energy changes with growth; I understand
we are not seeing eye-to-eye
disagreements
will happen
acceptance
something necessary
we can improve on
happy with our talks lately, but
you may not like what I have to say
breaking the habit of remaining mute
I got a voice; use it
channel surfing for good news
can't find any
unfazed by commotion
you can't comprehend
numb to negativity and

actions tell me everything
approach conversation with respect
cut you off like a single fabric string
embrace your acts of betrayal, or
I believe the worst will never happen
and we will always make amends

Genre: Reverse Poem
Theme: Life

"Adjustment"

I am sad
It is not true that
I believe that constant happiness
Is unrealistic
I had no choice but to accept my path
I am lost in a new place
nothing is the same because
Gloominess
Is a feeling stronger than
Jubilation
Some time ago
My soul was light
But lately, I have felt different
change has brought insecurity
Life will always have problems
However, I do not agree that

Smiles will radiate from my face
As the years fly by
I will sink into melancholy
Never will it be determined that
People will understand
It will be evident that sadness is inevitable
It is ridiculous to assume that
I will never be unhappy
And all of this will come true unless I reverse it

Genre: autobiographical
Theme: origin

"where I'm from"

I'm from a home of unconditional love and
support
enjoying days of laughter and evenings of
memories
competitive family fun blessed with home-
cooked meals
many can't relate to where I'm from

I am from the city of Tracy, California
not born but raised around the fields of farmers
running home before the bright street lights
flicker
growing up without a worry in the world

I'm from basketball courts where it's me vs.
everybody
thriving under pressure like larry bird in crunch
time
inspired by music hip-hop and r&b legends
like the mime, I'm the black sheep

I'm from the mind of hopeless romanticism
searching for a friend first, then a partner second

writing is the therapy that cures heartbreak
don't think I've met the one yet, or maybe I have

I'm from the mentality that success is the best
medicine
working hard to a fault, steadily improving on my
rest
dreaming big while making money manifesting
as we speak
mom always tells me, "patience is a virtue."

I'm from an island where the hidden treasure is
my thoughts
being lost in imagination, floating on the boat of
knowledge
I'm from a place where I'm just like mom and
dad
my heroes

Genre: Autobiographical
Theme: Origin

"Where I'm From"

I am from luck, planning, or divine intervention -
thankful that fate intervened and I was delivered into the
arms of Sam and Winnie.
I am from 3,000 miles away, a hardy, non-diverse state,
one in which snow drifts melt into humid thunderstorms.
I have visions of sledding down our hill on red saucers and
making snow angels,
and walking with my dog, Buttons, along our sharp-
edged shore of freezing Atlantic water.
I am from my Nana's garden of sweet peas and
cucumbers
and the ocean's gifts of lobster and clams caught that day
off the shore.
I am from the positivity umbrella, covering me when
times get tough,
allowing me to dream in color.
I have visions of my parents believing in me,
strengthening me for life to come
with the "You can do anything you set your mind to...."
mantra.
I am from that thick Maine accent asking someone to
"Pahk the cah...".
I have lived on the West Coast for many decades,
but the East Coast girl is still in me.

Made in the USA
Middletown, DE
06 June 2023

32149405R10038